COACH YOURSELF
BETTER, FAST

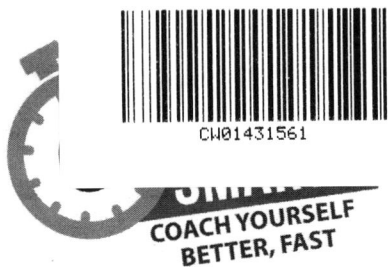

MANAGING BIG TEAMS

Based on *Big Teams* by Tony Llewellyn

First published in Great Britain by Practical Inspiration Publishing, 2025

ISBN   978-1-78860-818-3   (paperback)
       978-1-78860-819-0   (ebook)

EU GPSR representative: LOGOS EUROPE, 9 rue Nicolas Poussin, LA ROCHELLE 17000, France Contact@ logoseurope.eu.

Want to bulk-buy copies of this book for your team and colleagues? We can customize the content and co-brand *Managing Big Teams* to suit your business's needs.

Please email info@practicalinspiration.com for more details.

Practical Inspiration Publishing™

Contents

Series introduction

Welcome to *6-Minute Smarts*!

This is a series of very short books with one simple purpose: to introduce you to ideas that can make life and work better, and to give you time and space to think about how those ideas might apply to *your* life and work.

Each book introduces you to ten powerful ideas, but ideas on their own are useless – that's why each idea is followed by self-coaching questions to help you work out the 'so what?' for you in just six minutes of exploratory writing. What's exploratory writing? It's the kind of writing you do just for yourself, fast and free, without worrying what anyone else thinks. It's not just about getting ideas out of your head and onto paper where you can see them; it's about finding new connections and insights as you write. This is where the magic happens.

Whatever you're facing, there's a *6-Minute Smarts* book just for you. And once you've learned how to coach yourself through a new idea, you'll be smarter for life.

Find out more...

Introduction

This book explores how to manage what I call a Big Team – a large, shifting collection of small teams working together on complex projects. It's designed for leaders who want to improve human collaboration at scale.

In the modern workplace, individuals rarely work in isolation but are grouped with other colleagues into notional teams. The degree to which these collections of individuals come together to work as an effective unit is a topic of significant interest both to organizations and to academics. Given the right conditions, people working in teams can often achieve amazing outcomes. However, they can just as easily devolve into dysfunctional groups.

There's been a great deal of research in recent years into the question of how to build an effective team. Most of the research into team performance has tended to focus on individual units of between 8 and 12 people. Less attention has been paid to what happens when there's a need to create a very large team of hundreds or even thousands of human beings, all focused on achieving the same outcome. This book fills that gap.

I've done a lot of research in this area, both as a practising consultant and a part-time academic. I've spent much of my career working in the construction industry where the word 'team' is often used to describe anyone involved at a particular moment in the development of a physical asset. As I shifted my career to become more focused on how to help teams work together more productively, it became clear to me that the people and the organizations involved in the construction process habitually operated in a way that was often dysfunctional. The desire to improve how such large project teams work has been one of the drivers for my continued interest in this field.

As I've expanded my research beyond the construction sector into major projects in other industries, it has been fascinating to see the consistency of the behaviours of humans working in large groups. I've found that irrespective of sector or specialization, people working in large complex projects demonstrate the same propensity for collaborative creativity on the one hand and disruptive conflict on the other.

In this book, I'll introduce you to the components that have been found to help improve the chances of success, by tapping into the human instinct to work in teams. I'll also help you understand the darker side of human nature, and how the impact of our disruptive tendencies can be diminished.

This book is for anyone who aspires to take on a leadership role in a major project. The concepts, observations and ideas are also likely to be of interest to anyone wanting to develop their skills as team coaches. I use the term project leader and project manager as the primary title, but the qualifying attribute is leadership in whatever form or whatever element of a role you may occupy.

My hope is that you'll be inspired to learn and develop a skill set that I believe will be critical to the world's ability to find answers to the growing need for sustainable infrastructure and technological change. As projects grow in size and complexity, the world needs people who are able to lead and manage the large collections of specialist teams working at scale.

Over the next ten chapters (ten days, if you fancy treating this as a minicourse), you're going to discover ten key principles of leading Big Teams more effectively and experiment with using them for yourself.

Let's go!

Day 1

Understanding the Big Team challenge

Large teams aren't just scaled-up versions of small teams. Their dynamics, structures and challenges are fundamentally different. Understanding these differences is the first step in becoming an effective Big Team leader.

What makes Big Teams different

Big Teams are an essential feature of modern working life. The tasks and challenges faced by people in organizations require the collective skills and knowledge of different people assembled into effective units. Humans have been adept at working cooperatively in groups for thousands of years but are also equally capable of finding reasons to disagree and disconnect from each other.

In the last 50 years or so, leaders and academics have tried to understand the factors that influence a team to achieve results beyond expectations or to fall into dysfunction. For those interested in teamwork and team development, there's plenty of material to explore. But most of the published research focuses on small teams; less attention has been paid to large, shifting project teams.

A Big Team is not a single unified unit. It's an organic collection of individuals and small groups whose roles and activities shift and change as the project progresses. Some people may be involved for the entire duration of the project; others may be active participants for a few days, weeks or months. The number of people involved will grow beyond the scale and control of an individual leader. And yet the performance of the whole system depends on the interactions between all its parts.

Why Big Teams struggle to perform well

Projects are temporary in nature. Project teams have a different set of internal dynamics, which can both positively and negatively affect how they function. They are often short-term assemblages of people brought together for a defined outcome, with individuals arriving from different organizations, disciplines and geographies. Most project teams have no shared history.

As projects scale up in terms of scope, budget and programme length, more people become involved. They will quickly reorganize themselves into sub-teams, which may be based around function, discipline or simply personal affinity. These teams then start to behave as semi-autonomous units. Without clear governance and strong behavioural norms, the danger is that these sub-teams disconnect from the whole.

Each of these sub-teams may behave like a silo. People from one team may have little knowledge of, or interaction with, colleagues in other teams. Different subcultures form. Coordination becomes more difficult. Misunderstandings multiply.

Leadership on large projects often assumes that if everyone is pointed at the same outcome they will naturally behave as a team. This is rarely true. While the overall objective may be clear, different parts of the system start to interpret it in subtly different ways. This leads to friction, duplication and delay.

What often emerges instead are independent units with limited collaboration and misaligned priorities.

Complexity, uncertainty and human behaviour

The modern project environment is shaped by complexity and uncertainty. Projects begin with a high degree of ambiguity. The desired outcome may be broadly defined, but many of the key decisions about how to get there are yet to be made.

Complexity can be understood as a situation in which there are many interconnected variables such as time, scope, budget, resources, stakeholder needs, etc. Each variable exerts pressure on the others in ways that are not immediately obvious. Complexity increases when multiple new technologies are being used, which must then learn to interface with each other; when fluidity of design makes it difficult to fix contracts; and when human decisions and behaviours cannot be predicted.

Social complexity adds another layer. Project team members are drawn from different social and organizational cultures. They arrive with different understandings of what constitutes good behaviour, reasonable working practice and effective communication. These differences rarely surface in the early stages but become apparent as pressure builds.

The temporary nature of projects, combined with their novelty and time pressure, often leads to a lack of investment in the human system. Teams are launched without sufficient effort to establish norms, build relationships or develop shared meaning.

Uncertainty is an inevitable feature of project life, in that all major projects start with a large number of decisions yet to be made and questions to be answered. Uncertainty also manifests itself in the continual, unpredictable shift of external influences of wider political, social and technical factors. Human beings dislike uncertainty, particularly in situations that feel threatening, and where possible will try to find ways to manage unknown factors.

Instead of eliminating uncertainty, leaders must develop the capacity to navigate it.

The three competencies of delivery

There are three primary elements to every project, each requiring a distinct area of competence:

- **Technical competence**: The knowledge and awareness of how components of the project are to be designed and assembled

- **Commercial competence**: The knowledge and awareness of issues around money, contracts and the identification and management of risk
- **Social competence**: The knowledge and awareness of how humans behave in groups and teams

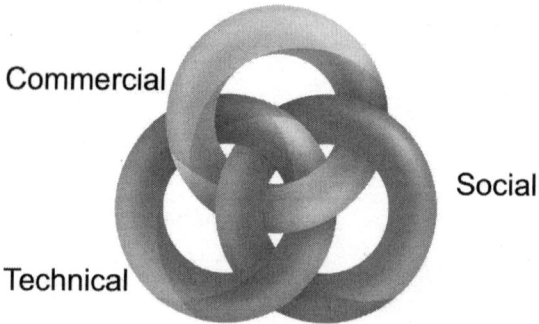

Commercial

Social

Technical

Figure 1.1 The three elements of project competence

Technical and commercial competencies are well understood and embedded in most project training programmes. Social competence is less well understood. It's rarely part of formal education or project management certification. And yet, it's often the critical differentiator between success and failure in large projects.

The capacity to manage the human system – to build trust, create alignment, and navigate conflict – is what enables the technical and commercial systems to function effectively.

The Big Team performance curve

At the start of a project, performance is typically low. Teams are forming, objectives are still being clarified and structures are still bedding in. As alignment improves and learning accelerates, performance increases. But unless engagement is sustained and resilience is supported, performance can begin to drop again.

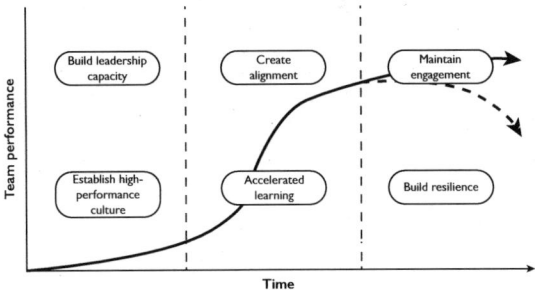

Figure 1.2 Team performance curve on complex projects

We're going to consider the key aspects of that journey towards creating a high-performing Big Team – one that can deliver in complex, dynamic conditions without burning out or falling apart.

So what? Over to you...

1. Where in my current team or project do I see signs of fragmentation or siloed behaviour?

2. How well do I balance technical, commercial and social competence in my leadership approach?

3. What assumptions am I making about how large teams should operate – and are they serving the project?

Day 2

The hidden rules
of big teaming

Big Teams don't fail because of incompetence. They fail because of misalignment – often driven by invisible assumptions about how people should behave. These 'hidden rules' shape everything, and left unexamined, they can erode performance from within.

Why behaviour in Big Teams often defaults to dysfunction

Many major projects begin with high ambition. A new team is formed, composed of people from different organizations, often with impressive credentials and experience. There's a sense of purpose and excitement.

However, within weeks or even days, problems start to appear. Meetings are tense or unproductive. Communication between teams is patchy. Decision making slows down. Blame begins to circulate.

The causes are rarely technical. They are behavioural. And the behaviours are not necessarily malicious or negligent – they are habitual.

People revert to what they know. They rely on past patterns, cultural defaults and learned self-protection. In the absence of clear shared norms, these defaults quickly harden into silos and friction.

The impact of unspoken rules

In many Big Teams, people operate according to hidden rules – assumptions about what is acceptable, expected or risky. These rules are rarely written down or discussed. They emerge from prior environments, personal experiences and unspoken norms.

Examples of hidden rules:

- Don't question senior leaders in meetings
- Only speak when you have a solution
- Keep problems within your own team
- Never admit mistakes unless you can blame someone else
- Wait to be told what to do.

These assumptions can be deeply embedded, and they vary from team to team. When multiple groups with different hidden rules come together in a single project, misunderstandings are inevitable.

Sometimes the rules are protective. People don't speak up because they fear being dismissed or judged. Sometimes they are strategic – teams protect their scope, control information or assert independence to gain influence.

Left unexamined, these rules shape culture in ways that no amount of process or structure can fix.

How high-performing teams behave

Google's Project Aristotle studied over 180 teams to understand what distinguished high performance. The findings were not about IQ, individual competence or management structures. They were about *behavioural norms*.

Five key variables emerged:

1. **Psychological safety**: Team members feel safe enough to take risks and be vulnerable in front of each other
2. **Dependability**: People can rely on each other to follow through

3. **Structure and clarity**: Roles, plans and expectations are clearly understood

4. **Meaning**: The work has personal significance to team members

5. **Impact**: The team believes that their work matters.

These five variables apply just as much to Big Teams as to smaller ones – but they must be actively cultivated. They do not arise automatically, especially when people come from different cultures and companies.

Teams that share these characteristics are more innovative, more resilient under pressure, and more able to collaborate across boundaries.

Making behavioural norms explicit

Culture is not something you impose. It emerges from repeated behaviours, shared experiences and what leaders tolerate, encourage or ignore.

A Big Team does not have a single homogeneous culture. Each small team will develop its own subculture. This is driven by the team's leaders, by the circumstances of the project and by the other social or commercial elements that tie them together.

However, project leadership *can* shape the environment in which culture emerges. This begins with making behavioural expectations explicit.

One leadership group created a set of team agreements in the first month of the programme. These included:

- We speak honestly and respectfully – even when it's hard
- We share problems early, before they become crises
- We assume positive intent
- We give and receive feedback regularly
- We support decisions once made – even if we disagreed.

These behaviours were co-created in a workshop setting. They were printed, shared and reinforced. When issues arose, the leadership team referred back to the agreements – not to punish, but to remind and reset.

This kind of clarity builds alignment across diverse teams. It creates a shared language and lowers the social cost of calling out unhelpful behaviour.

When behavioural norms are left to chance, each team operates to its own standard. The result is misunderstanding, conflict and disengagement.

The role of leadership in shaping culture

Leaders shape culture by what they model, what they prioritize and how they respond to deviation. In complex, fast-paced projects, leadership is often stretched thin. The temptation is to focus on deliverables and defer culture to 'later'.

But culture is not optional. It's the system through which performance happens – or doesn't.

Green-stage leaders devote time and attention to establishing shared values. They don't assume alignment – they build it. They understand that culture arises through hundreds of small actions: how meetings are run, how decisions are made, how feedback is handled, how conflict is resolved.

They also recognize that culture must be adaptive. As projects evolve, teams change. New people arrive, old patterns return. Cultural alignment is a constant process, not a one-time event.

In one programme, the leadership team embedded monthly check-ins to ask: 'What behaviours are helping us deliver? Which ones are getting in the way?' This simple prompt surfaced hidden tensions and allowed for course correction – before problems became embedded.

So what? Over to you...

1. What 'unspoken rules' seem to govern how my teams behave – especially under pressure?

2. Where might those rules be holding back collaboration or trust?

3. What small changes could I make to reinforce more constructive behavioural norms?

Day 3
The five levels of team interaction

Most project leaders look at the org chart and think they understand how their team works. But Big Teams aren't flat systems – they are layered human networks. Performance is shaped by how people interact across five distinct levels.

Why structure alone isn't enough

Large project teams are often treated as a single unit. Charts show a clean hierarchy or matrix. Job titles and reporting lines are defined. Everyone is 'on the team'.

But day-to-day collaboration happens elsewhere – in side conversations, ad hoc working groups and informal alliances. And that means the real team system is more complex, and more fragile, than it looks on paper.

Big Teams succeed when the relationships within and between sub-units function well. They struggle when communication breaks down at key touchpoints. The task of leadership is to understand and support these hidden patterns of connection.

The five nested levels of interaction

In any Big Team, there are at least five levels of human connection:

1. **Individual**: A person's values, energy, emotional state and ability to self-regulate
2. **Dyad**: The connection between two people, often a manager and a direct report or two collaborators who rely on each other
3. **Workgroup**: A small group of people who share a task or deliverable, e.g. a planning team, engineering team or commercial team
4. **Team**: A larger cluster of workgroups brought together for a shared outcome, typically part of a major project stage

5. **Project:** The whole system, comprising all individuals, workgroups and teams across the programme.

The small team is the unit of production within any large enterprise. Emperors and generals have historically organized their armies and administrators into manageable groups. This is not, however, a top-down management strategy to create neatly arranged grouping on an org chart. It's actually a reflection of how humans prefer to work with each other.

Humans can typically maintain strong working relationships with 6 to 10 people. Once a team exceeds this size, sub-grouping occurs naturally. This is not a problem – but it must be managed.

Real teams vs pseudo teams

Not all groups that call themselves 'teams' behave like one. Jon Katzenbach and Douglas Smith defined a real team as:

> A small number of people with complementary skills who are committed to a common purpose, performance goals and approach for which they hold themselves mutually accountable.[1]

In contrast:

- A **working group** shares an interest but not a common goal or joint accountability.
- A **pseudo team** wants to be seen as a real team but lacks trust, shared ownership or collaborative behaviour.

Pseudo teams can form quickly on large projects – especially when individuals are co-located but not aligned. They may meet regularly, use team language and coordinate on paper, but avoid honest feedback, resist shared responsibility and fall back on blame.

Effective leadership distinguishes between team form and team function – and takes deliberate steps to support real teaming.

Sub-teams, silos and cohesion

Sub-teams develop their own identities. These are shaped by history (teams who've worked together before), discipline (engineering, design, procurement) or company culture (joint ventures, subcontractors, internal/external mixes).

Each small team will develop its own subculture. This is driven by the team's leaders, by the circumstances of the project and by the other social or commercial elements that tie them together.

When sub-teams align with each other, the larger system works. When they diverge, fragmentation sets in. People focus inward. Assumptions go unchallenged. Frustration grows.

It's tempting to treat cohesion as a personality issue – 'these two teams just don't get along.' But more often, it's a systems issue. Lack of cross-team visibility, unclear interfaces, inconsistent communication and absent shared goals all lead to silos.

Some sub-teams thrive in this environment – because they isolate themselves from dysfunction. But this is short-term success at the cost of the larger mission.

Building performance at every level

You cannot make a Big Team work simply by appointing a strong leader and hoping the rest falls into place. High performance must be supported at *every level.*

At the **individual** level:

• Leaders model openness, regulate their stress responses and manage their energy

28

- Team members understand their role and value within the bigger picture.

At the **dyad** level:

- Key relationships (e.g. project manager and planner, design and construction leads) are strong enough to surface disagreement constructively
- Conflict is addressed, not avoided.

At the **workgroup** level:

- Teams have clear objectives, routines, feedback loops and autonomy
- The team identity is strong, but not insular.

At the **team** level:

- Multiple workgroups coordinate without needing constant escalation
- Interface risks are actively managed, not just tracked.

At the **project** level:

- The leadership group ensures alignment across the programme
- There's shared ownership for the health of the whole system.

A breakdown at any level affects the next. If individuals are over-stretched, dyads falter. If dyads are adversarial, workgroups lose cohesion. If workgroups are siloed, project-level integration fails.

The ripple effect of weak links

On a major infrastructure project, I worked with a leadership team who initially saw the root cause of programme delays as external – supplier underperformance, weather issues, regulatory bottlenecks.

But a closer look revealed that one internal team was failing to deliver consistent outputs. This team had unclear objectives, frequent turnover and low morale. Other teams were forced to compensate, leading to missed milestones elsewhere.

For many large projects, the ability to stay on programme will be governed by the weakest team. I've seen large projects put under pressure by a single team that had started to fail and needed 'rescuing' by other teams working in that phase of the works. Conversely, when every team is working as an effective unit, I've heard of projects surging forward and delivering ahead of schedule.

The lesson: a Big Team only performs at the level of its least-supported component. Fixing the system means paying attention to every layer.

✏️ So what? Over to you...

1. Which levels of interaction in my Big Team receive regular attention – and which are ignored?

2. Are any of my sub-teams pseudo teams? What evidence supports that?

3. Where could early signs of underperformance in one group ripple across the project?

Day 4
Clarifying purpose and meaning

Purpose in a Big Team is not just a motivational slogan. It's the anchor that holds diverse groups together when things become complex or uncertain. Without shared purpose, alignment frays and momentum stalls.

How shared purpose gives cohesion to large teams

When working with project leaders, I frequently hear the desire to create a high-performing team, without having a clear idea as to what high performance actually entails. What constitutes performance is subjective, depending upon the expectations of a particular team. When working with a collection of teams that make up a Big Team, performance must be articulated much more clearly so that there's a common understanding by everyone involved as to what is expected. The performance of a team of teams will tend to be tied to the ability of each sub-team to operate successfully. The more aligned they are around a common purpose, the greater the likelihood of success.

Clarifying purpose means helping people understand the 'why' of the work – not just the what or how. If purpose is not clear, or is interpreted differently by each team, the project loses cohesion. Individual teams may optimize their own outputs while undermining the system as a whole.

There's a big difference between output and purpose. One is about activity, the other is about impact. A team may complete a report or submit a design without understanding why it matters, or how it connects to the bigger picture. This disconnect reduces engagement, creativity and ownership.

Meaningful engagement beyond tasks

When we feel positive about our work and have a sense of progression, we will put in additional discretionary effort and creative problem-solving. On the other hand, if we feel remote from the project leadership and do not feel informed about what is happening elsewhere, we can quickly fall into a state of apathy.

Meaning and impact were two of the five key variables identified in Google's Project Aristotle study. When people believe their work matters – and aligns with their values – they give more of themselves to the task. This is especially true on long or complex projects, where daily work can feel disconnected from final outcomes.

Some Big Teams try to create motivation through financial incentives or performance bonuses. But these mechanisms only go so far. What really drives sustained engagement is emotional commitment to a shared goal. People need to know they are contributing to something worthwhile.

One senior leader in a transport programme described the difference as 'getting people to work for a cause, not just a contract'. He spent the first six months of the programme visiting every team, sharing the broader vision, listening to concerns and asking how their work aligned with the customer's needs. He credits this work with creating the trust that held the team together through a tough delivery phase.

Vision, values and direction of travel

Large projects usually begin with a high degree of uncertainty in that while the desired outcome is broadly understood, the exact mechanisms required to get there have yet to be conceived. Having many small teams each trying to work out their own interpretation of what will be required is likely to result in chaos.

Big Teams must therefore be able to focus on the right direction of travel even if they are not yet clear on the exact route. This is where vision becomes powerful – not as lofty language, but as a guide to shared judgement. A clear and credible vision allows people to make good decisions in the absence of detailed instruction. It creates alignment without micromanagement.

Green leadership teams devote a lot of time to articulating and then reinforcing the values that should be adopted. They also carefully pay attention to wider stakeholder concerns. Values act as a compass. They guide behaviour in the grey areas – how we treat each other under pressure, how we manage trade-offs, how we respond to challenge.

In one major infrastructure project, the leadership team used five short value statements to anchor every induction and team meeting. These included

'We act in service of the whole,' 'We challenge with respect' and 'We take ownership of outcomes.' These statements became a shared reference point when tensions rose or decisions were disputed.

Without these anchors, different teams develop their own interpretations of success. Some optimize for speed, others for quality, others for visibility. This misalignment can cause conflict, rework and lost momentum.

James's story: shifting from control to shared purpose

The programme was a multi-million-dollar technology project requiring the integration of multiple teams with different specialties and organizational cultures. The initial project director was highly experienced but took an 'old school' view of leadership – centralized control, tight command and minimal engagement. He quickly became unpopular. Sub-teams began to work in isolation. Communication broke down. Trust eroded.

Eventually this individual moved on. The leadership group that took over included James, a systems engineer with a strong interest in collaborative working. James worked with his colleagues to explore an alternative approach. They decided to break down the traditional hub-and-spoke relationship in which the leadership team sat at the centre and passed out instructions to other teams. Instead, they shifted responsibility to the edges.

Each sub-team took accountability for its deliverables. The leadership group focused on enabling alignment and facilitating communication across boundaries. Face-to-face meetings were introduced between team leaders. Programme goals were redefined in terms of customer value, not just technical milestones.

The tone of interaction changed. Problems were surfaced earlier. Solutions were developed collaboratively. Relationships improved. The programme remained on track despite several external disruptions.

This shift from control to shared purpose allowed the team of teams to function as a coherent, adaptive system. It required courage, patience and a commitment to values – but the results were clear.

Making purpose real at all levels

Clarifying purpose is not a one-time exercise. It must be revisited regularly, especially as the project evolves.

New people join, priorities shift and external factors create uncertainty. Leaders must re-anchor teams in the 'why'.

Purpose can be made tangible in everyday actions:

- In planning meetings, frame tasks in terms of their impact
- In onboarding, connect roles to the bigger picture
- In feedback conversations, link performance to shared values
- In cross-team forums, celebrate contributions that support the whole
- In retrospectives, reflect on what mattered – not just what got done.

These practices turn abstract vision into daily meaning. They help each person see how their work contributes to something beyond their immediate deliverables. And that sense of connection drives commitment, resilience and innovation.

✏️ So what? Over to you...

1. How do I make the purpose of our work clear, credible and motivating to all teams?

2. Do I emphasize values and vision early enough to shape behaviour?

3. Where and how might individuals feel disconnected from the larger goal?

Day 5
Designing structures for collaboration

Big Teams don't just need structure – they need structures that support collaboration, not just control. Formal systems provide clarity, but it's informal networks that carry most of the load. Both need careful design.

Formal structures: governance, roles and communication

Big Teams demand structure. Without it, ambiguity spreads and duplication thrives. People don't know who to ask, who makes decisions, or how information flows. Energy is lost to confusion.

Designing structures for collaboration

The challenge is to create structures that provide direction and stability without becoming rigid or hierarchical. This requires clarity about:

- Who has authority to make what decisions
- How teams interface with one another
- What routines support coordination and information sharing
- How progress is monitored and accountability is maintained.

An effective set-up programme creates the conditions for:

- Clear objectives fixed around sponsor and customer needs
- Low hierarchy allowing direct connections
- High accountability within a low-blame culture
- Fluid peer-to-peer networks
- Strong behavioural norms that support collaboration.

In some programmes, this means designing not just the reporting lines, but the rhythm of meetings, the cadence of reviews and the expectations around communication. Too often, these elements are left to emerge on their own – leading to uneven coordination and local improvisation.

Informal structures: relationships, influence and trust

Structure isn't just about boxes and arrows, it's about relationships – the informal connections that allow people to get work done across boundaries. People don't always solve problems by escalating through the hierarchy. They solve them by calling someone they trust.

In practice, informal networks carry more influence than many formal systems. But informal networks are only productive when trust is high and expectations are shared.

In James's story above, the leadership group deliberately chose not to act as a central bottleneck. Instead of requiring all communication to route through a project manager, they enabled direct communication between teams. Responsibility was distributed. Interfaces were managed through weekly team leader forums. The leadership group focused on alignment and support.

This shift had significant consequences. Sub-teams took more ownership. Communication was faster. Blame was replaced with shared problem-solving. Performance improved.

This was not the result of a clever org chart, it was the outcome of a conscious choice to trust the system – supported by structures that encouraged autonomy and coordination, not control.

Structural enablers: forums, admin support and routines

One of the major factors influencing collaboration is the availability of shared space – physical or virtual – where teams can meet, exchange information and manage interdependencies. In successful projects, structured interaction between teams is not left to chance.

In James's programme, face-to-face meetings were used early in the mobilization phase to agree behaviours, clarify roles and define boundaries. These meetings brought together people from multiple workstreams and allowed misunderstandings to surface early. They also helped build rapport that would support collaboration later.

The programme also invested in administrative staff to support coordination. These individuals were not senior technical specialists, but graduate-level professionals who understood project processes and could facilitate communication. Their role was to keep the programme organized – scheduling meetings, maintaining interface registers, supporting decision logs and tracking actions.

Rather than being a side role for highly qualified engineers, the joint programme office (JPO) employed individuals who were more effective in enabling collaboration across the whole programme. This freed up the technical leaders to focus on delivery, while improving overall connectivity.

This kind of operational support is often undervalued. But in Big Teams, where the volume of coordination required is high, it can make the difference between reactive firefighting and proactive delivery.

Designing connection across boundaries

It's easy to forget that structure affects how people feel. In poorly designed systems, teams feel isolated or micromanaged. In well-designed systems, teams feel supported and empowered.

Key structural design questions include:

- Are decision rights clear, and located as close to delivery as possible?
- Are interfaces mapped and owned, or assumed?

- Are regular touchpoints in place across boundaries, not just up and down lines?
- Is there administrative support to help the right conversations happen at the right time?
- Are routines in place to catch misalignment early?

When teams are forced to invent their own systems, they often optimize for themselves. This can lead to duplication, turf wars and disengagement. By contrast, when structures are designed to encourage lateral communication and shared accountability, teams collaborate more readily and deliver more reliably.

Balance is critical. Too much structure stifles initiative. Too little invites chaos. The right amount enables people to coordinate effectively while adapting locally.

Structures as evolving systems

Project structures must evolve over time. What works in mobilization may not work during peak delivery or close-out. As the team grows and contracts, structures need to be reviewed and revised.

In one programme, the leadership team conducted a quarterly review of its governance, forums and communications routines. As the project shifted from design to construction, they reduced formal review meetings and increased co-location. They also adapted roles and decision rights to suit new priorities.

This responsiveness helped maintain alignment. Teams did not experience major shocks or prolonged confusion. They adjusted with the system.

Structures are not static. They are part of the delivery system. Leaders must design them, use them and update them as the project evolves.

🖉 So what? Over to you...

1. Are our current structures helping or hindering collaboration?

---

2. Do informal networks align with formal roles – or bypass them?

3. Where could I improve how teams connect without adding bureaucracy?

Day 6
Working with team dynamics

Structure and clarity matter. But in a Big Team, what really determines success is how people behave – especially under pressure. Team dynamics are where plans meet reality.

Recognizing and managing interpersonal tensions in large teams

The ability of humans to cooperate with each other is hard wired into our genetic framework. We have survived and thrived as a species because we can work together to share labour, protect each other and pool our knowledge and ideas. This does not, however, mean that we are naturally good at teamwork. We also have an innate tendency to compete with each other.

You don't need to be an expert in behavioural science to recognize that people are not automatically programmed to communicate effectively with others they do not know. Simply assembling a large group of people and expecting them to work as a collective unit is unlikely to produce an instantly organized and focused team.

If the social system in which individuals operate is actively and thoughtfully managed, this can produce a rich network of collaborative effort. If left to chance, there's likely to be a slow descent into a 'them and us' blame game.

One team I worked with experienced exactly this descent. They started out with optimism, but within three months communication was limited to formal meetings. Informal dialogue stopped. Frustration rose. The technical work was sound, but relationships were strained. The team lead admitted, 'We thought we were aligned. Turns out we'd never really talked about how we'd work together.'

Trust and psychological safety

Psychological safety – the sense that it's safe to speak up, ask questions and admit mistakes – is the foundation of effective team dynamics. It's also the variable most often missing on underperforming Big Teams.

One of the critical variables identified by Google's Project Aristotle was psychological safety – the sense that people feel safe enough to take risks and be vulnerable in each other's presence. Without psychological safety people will play it safe, remain silent, avoid responsibility and take as few risks as possible.

In large, fast-forming teams, there's often no time to develop trust slowly. Trust is a decision. If the conditions are right, people will give it – if not, they won't. Trust accelerates performance; its absence creates drag.

Leaders often assume they will build trust over time. But the scale and speed of most projects require trust to be offered up front, not earned incrementally. This means setting conditions that make trust rational.

Key signs of low trust include:

- Meetings where no one raises concerns
- Decisions made without consultation
- Blame for delays passed between teams
- People saying 'yes' in meetings but acting differently later.

Trust is fragile, and when broken it takes time to repair. But it can also be strengthened quickly through transparency, consistency and follow-through.

Behavioural norms and their enforcement

Without a clear agreement around behaviours, each individual will be guided by their previous experiences and personal preferences. In large projects, this often leads to clashes between multiple interpretations of acceptable conduct.

The more rapidly the team has been assembled, the greater the likelihood that norms will be assumed rather than articulated. The absence of behavioural clarity usually manifests in interpersonal friction. People begin to complain about meetings, avoid collaboration or 'go dark' when things go wrong.

Green-stage teams are deliberate about co-designing behavioural expectations. In one programme, senior leaders and frontline staff participated together in a series of workshops to define shared commitments. These included:

- We address issues early, not late
- We assume positive intent
- We share responsibility for outcomes
- We speak directly, not about each other.

These norms were displayed visibly in team spaces, referenced in meetings and used in performance conversations. They were not framed as rules, but as a shared standard of conduct.

When behavioural norms are co-created and consistently reinforced, teams become more resilient. They can navigate tension without breaking down. They can push for performance without triggering defensiveness.

Modelling the right behaviours

It's not enough to state expectations; leaders must model them.

One project director began each team meeting by sharing a mistake he'd made that week, and what he'd learned from it. His goal was to normalize openness and demonstrate that learning mattered more than blame.

Another leadership team reviewed its own behaviours every month, using a short survey and open discussion. They asked: 'Where did we live our values? Where did we fall short?' This visible self-accountability made it safer for others to speak up.

When leaders model curiosity, transparency and humility, they make it easier for teams to follow suit.

When they model defensiveness, blame or avoidance, those become the norms.

In Big Teams, people watch leadership closely. They will not always do what leaders say – but they will often do what leaders do.

Dealing with disruption early

Poor team dynamics rarely fix themselves. Without attention, they worsen. Frustrations build. Small issues escalate. People withdraw or act out. Recovery becomes harder.

One leadership group noticed that two workstream leads had stopped engaging in meetings. Rather than ignore it, the sponsor invited them to a short conversation, not to critique, but to ask: 'What's going on, and how can we support you better?' It turned out they felt excluded from key decisions. With that surfaced, the group adjusted its processes and rebuilt trust.

Disruption is not always a sign of failure. It can be a sign that something important needs attention. But only if the team has the safety and skills to surface and respond to it.

Behavioural drift is natural. Without reinforcement, teams move away from agreed norms. That's why regular reflection, feedback and re-commitment are essential.

In Big Teams, team dynamics are not just a human resources concern; they are a core delivery factor.

✏️ So what? Over to you…

1. Where do I see signs of psychological safety – or fear – in our team dynamics?

---

2. Are our behavioural expectations clear, shared and reinforced?

3. Where might a more structured conversation help realign relationships?

Day 7
Leading in complexity

In Big Teams, leadership isn't about control – it's about creating the conditions for others to succeed. Complexity demands distributed ownership, adaptive response and a shift in mindset from hero to host.

Leadership as context, not control

The commonly understood concept of leadership is that it's a set of qualities possessed by an individual who directs and motivates a group toward a particular objective. However, successful leadership is less about the individual, and more about the context of the group and how it functions as an effective unit.

The traditional 'hero leader' struggles in complex, dynamic project environments. These environments are too fast, too uncertain and too interconnected for one person to direct every decision. Central control slows things down. Frontline teams wait for approval, escalate issues and disengage from ownership.

The role of leadership in a Big Team is to shape context – to design the systems, behaviours and relationships that allow distributed teams to align, adapt and deliver. It's not about removing uncertainty. It's about helping the team to navigate it.

On one programme, the project director described his role as 'gardener, not general'. His job was not to issue orders, but to prepare the ground – clearing obstacles, encouraging growth and helping others take root.

Leading through complexity means enabling, not directing.

Adaptive leadership and the team of leaders

Leadership in a Big Team is never just one person. It's the product of many people stepping into leadership roles, formally or informally. This is why I prefer to work with the idea of a leadership group.

Within this group there will be the project director, sponsor, programme manager and a range of other people with formal leadership roles. Around them is a wider group of informal leaders, such as technical experts, workstream leads and advisors, who influence how the project works.

Adaptive leadership is not a fixed style. It's a way of responding to changing conditions. Sometimes directive, sometimes coaching, sometimes stepping back to observe. The key is responsiveness – not to mood, but to context.

In one major programme, the leadership group dedicated time each week to reflect – not just on outputs, but on team dynamics. They asked questions like 'What's changing?', 'What tensions are emerging?' and 'Where do we need to adjust?'

This reflection allowed them to pivot quickly when priorities shifted. When a major supply chain disruption hit, they moved from 'monitoring progress' to 'supporting decision making at the edges'. They didn't try to solve everything. They enabled teams to take the lead.

This adaptability was not accidental. It was built into the system.

Shifting from control to ownership

James's story (introduced in earlier chapters) offers a clear illustration of this shift. Initially, the programme was led by a director who favoured command and control. Information flowed inward. Decisions flowed outward. Sub-teams became passive, waiting for direction. Communication broke down. Morale dropped.

Eventually, the leadership changed. James and his colleagues replaced the hub-and-spoke model with a networked system. Each team owned its scope. The leadership group acted as a facilitator – connecting teams, clarifying priorities and enabling peer collaboration.

Responsibility shifted. Meetings became more productive. Leaders emerged at all levels. Problems were surfaced earlier and solved faster.

This shift wasn't just structural – it was cultural. It required the leadership group to let go of control, trust the system and support learning. But the payoff was significant: higher engagement, faster delivery and a stronger team culture.

Shared leadership is not abdication. It's amplification. When the system is trusted and supported, it performs better than any single individual could direct.

Post-heroic leadership and vulnerability

The post-heroic leader does not try to be the smartest person in the room. Instead, they create space for others to contribute, challenge and lead.

This requires vulnerability. It means saying 'I don't know' or 'What do you think?' It means admitting when things aren't working and inviting others into the solution.

Green-stage leaders model this behaviour consistently. They share responsibility for results. They coach others to lead. They invite feedback. They acknowledge uncertainty.

One sponsor I worked with regularly shared with their leadership team what they were learning – and where they were struggling. This openness changed the tone of the group. Others began to speak more honestly. Risks were raised earlier. Reflection became routine.

When leaders admit gaps, it gives others permission to do the same. When they pretend to have all the answers, silence becomes the norm.

Leadership in Big Teams is less about being right and more about being real.

Creating leadership conditions across the project

Leadership must be distributed – but it must also be supported. People will not step up if they feel exposed or undermined. They need conditions that allow them to lead well.

These include:

- Clarity of scope and expectations
- Psychological safety to speak, experiment and learn
- Access to information and feedback
- Support from peers and senior leaders
- Recognition of effort and shared success.

One project created a 'peer leader network' – a group of team leads from different disciplines who met fortnightly to share challenges, swap tools and offer support. This informal forum became a critical enabler of shared leadership. It reduced isolation, built trust and surfaced system-wide issues before they escalated.

Leadership is a team function. It works best when leaders support each other, share context and model aligned behaviours.

So what? Over to you...

1. Where might I be trying to lead alone instead of with others?

2. How does our leadership group respond to uncertainty – adaptively or defensively?

3. What one shift could I make to support shared ownership this week?

Day 8
Building and sustaining relationships

Big Teams run on relationships. Without strong connections across the system, communication breaks down, trust evaporates and delivery suffers. Investing in relationships is not a side task – it's central to performance.

Why relationships drive performance

The complexity and scale of modern project environments are beyond the ability of any one person to understand or control. As a result, more people need to be involved and more effort must be made to develop the social capital within the team.

When teams know each other personally, they share more information, cooperate more readily and are more willing to offer and ask for help. The hidden cost of poor relationships is delay, miscommunication, duplication and blame.

In the military, teamwork can be a matter of life and death. Huge amounts of time and resource are devoted to training and team development. In civilian projects, we often assume people will just 'get along'.

This assumption is dangerous – especially when people come from different companies, disciplines and cultures.

Control slows things down. Relationships speed them up. When relationships are strong, coordination becomes easier. Misunderstandings are resolved before they become conflicts. Resources are shared more flexibly. People speak more honestly and take more ownership.

In one programme, strong relationships between design and construction teams helped avoid weeks of delay. Instead of following escalation protocols, team leads resolved the issue in a quick informal meeting – because they trusted each other.

The cost of neglecting relationships

When relationships are weak, people avoid difficult conversations. They defer decisions or make them in isolation. They duplicate effort, protect turf and withhold information. Confidence drops. Blame increases.

I've seen projects where technical capability was high but performance was low – simply because the teams didn't talk to each other. Interfaces were managed through documents, not dialogue. Collaboration was transactional. When problems arose, people retreated into defensiveness.

In one case, poor relationships between the engineering and commercial teams led to conflicting priorities. Design decisions were made without full commercial implications being understood. This created scope gaps, contract disputes and rework. None of it was about competence. It was about connection.

Designing for connection

Good relationships don't happen by chance. They must be designed for.

This includes:

- Creating time and space for people to build trust
- Structuring forums for cross-team dialogue
- Encouraging informal interactions, not just formal meetings
- Supporting the people who connect the system – interface managers, coordinators, facilitators.

In James's programme, cross-functional relationships were deliberately nurtured. Team leaders were given time to build trust through informal conversations as well as formal meetings. The results were visible in delivery: faster, smoother, less adversarial.

Where there was no time for connection, people became territorial and disengaged. One leader described it as 'teams protecting their patch, not delivering the programme'.

Practical strategies to support relationship-building

Some Big Team strategies that support relationship-building include:

- Cross-team forums focused on shared challenges
- Regular, in-person meetings during critical phases
- Deliberate pairing of teams with interface dependencies
- A 'buddy system' between adjacent disciplines or contractors
- Visible leadership presence in day-to-day working areas
- Shared reflection sessions after key milestones.

One programme introduced a monthly 'interface walk' where leaders from two neighbouring teams visited each other's workspaces. They walked through progress, flagged issues and shared feedback. These simple visits improved mutual understanding and reduced tensions.

Another project ran informal end-of-week gatherings, open to all team members. These were not status updates. They were social check-ins – an opportunity to connect, appreciate effort and stay grounded in the shared mission.

These strategies are not about being 'nice'. They are about building the connective tissue that allows a complex system to move as one.

Supporting the connectors

In every Big Team, there are individuals who serve as informal bridges. These may be interface managers, workstream leads, admin coordinators or site supervisors. Their job is not to control – it's to connect.

These people often work behind the scenes. They notice gaps, smooth tensions and translate between different groups. But they are rarely recognized or supported.

In successful programmes, the leadership group invests in these roles. They provide training, visibility and legitimacy. They create spaces where these individuals can share insight and get support.

One project created a coordination forum specifically for these 'connectors'. It became a hub of early warning signals, practical ideas and relationship repair.

If ignored, these people burn out or disengage. If supported, they amplify team resilience.

Maintaining relationships under pressure

Relationships are easy to build when things are going well. The test comes under pressure.

Building and sustaining relationships

Big Teams need practices that sustain relationships through the hard times. These include:

- Reaffirming shared goals when tension rises
- Naming the difficulty without assigning blame
- Returning to shared values and behavioural norms
- Prioritizing face-to-face conversation over email escalation
- Taking time to repair trust when it's been damaged.

One leadership team paused a project review meeting when it became clear that two senior leads were in conflict. Rather than push through, they brought the leads together the next morning to talk. A facilitator supported the conversation. The issue was surfaced, heard and resolved. That moment prevented a rift from spreading through the wider team.

Strong relationships don't mean absence of conflict. They mean the ability to work through conflict constructively.

So what? Over to you...

1. Where are relationships strong – and where are they missing?

2. Have I designed time and space for informal connection, or am I relying on chance?

3. What one step could I take this week to deepen trust across a key interface?

Day 9

Diagnosing problems and stuck patterns

Even well-designed Big Teams get stuck. Diagnosing what's wrong – and where – requires awareness, reflection and sensitivity to both human and systemic signals. Recovery starts with clarity.

Recognizing signs of dysfunction in Big Teams

Dysfunction creeps in over time. You may hear people start to complain that other teams are not pulling their weight. Blame starts to get assigned to people or groups who are 'not on the bus'. There's more talk about who should have done what than there is about the next set of actions. Meeting conversations become more formal and less productive.

When a Big Team is working well, there's a collective buzz and a sense that the team is achieving something special. When the mood shifts, people become withdrawn, quiet and occasionally aggressive.

Communication between teams becomes inconsistent, partial or overly formal. People stop offering discretionary effort. Initiative is replaced by defensiveness.

These symptoms are often rationalized as 'normal growing pains' – but they are signs of stuck patterns that need attention.

In one project, a series of missed milestones led to public blame between two partner organizations. The leadership team initially treated the issue as technical – an issue of scope and sequencing. But it became clear that the problem was deeper: trust had broken down and teams had stopped talking to each other. A behavioural issue had become a delivery risk.

Using reflection and feedback to surface unseen issues

One of the challenges in identifying and correcting dysfunction in a Big Team is that most of the communication between individuals is transient. The world of projects is full of meetings, phone calls and emails that flow between people as they interact. It's not therefore easy to spot where the problems are developing, as so much of what happens is intangible.

One technique I've used to gather useful information about the state of the team is to ask team members to complete a short questionnaire. The results are then used to inform conversations about what is working and what is not.

The power of these surveys is in the patterns, not the scores. High variance may indicate alignment issues. Repeated low trust scores in one part of the team may suggest a leadership or cultural gap.

Structured reflection – at key milestones or moments of tension – creates space to talk about what's below the surface. A simple routine such as 'What's working? What's not? What do we need to change?' can surface issues early.

In one project, the leadership group held monthly retrospectives. These short sessions were used not only to track progress, but also to ask how people were feeling and where friction was building. The conversations weren't always comfortable – but they revealed what the metrics missed.

Where projects avoided this kind of reflection, misalignment lingered until it showed up in slippage, turnover or escalation.

Intervention strategies that respect scale and complexity

Effective interventions in Big Teams respect both scale and complexity. They are rarely about issuing instructions or conducting mass workshops. Instead, they rely on:

- Creating safe spaces for dialogue
- Identifying the small number of high-leverage shifts that will unlock progress
- Using leaders as multipliers, not bottlenecks.

For example, one project leadership group held a series of small team-based workshops to explore how their behaviours impacted others. Each group included members from adjacent workstreams. The process wasn't expensive or complicated – but it significantly improved communication and reduced conflict at key interfaces.

Another programme invested in short coaching sessions for key leaders. The goal wasn't personal development – it was diagnosis. Each leader was asked

'What's stuck in your area?', 'What's the conversation no one is having?' and 'What needs to shift?'

These conversations helped the leadership group spot patterns and design focused interventions.

The mistake many leaders make is to go too big, too fast – launching grand change programmes that create more churn than clarity.

Small changes, repeated consistently, shape culture.

Avoiding escalation paralysis

In a stuck system, escalation becomes the default. When teams can't resolve issues locally, they pass them up. This creates delay, adds stress to senior leaders and disempowers teams.

In some projects, escalation becomes cultural: people wait to be told, avoid hard conversations or assume someone else will fix the issue.

To avoid escalation paralysis:

- Ensure interface owners have clear authority and support
- Reinforce local problem-solving before escalation
- Make time to review how escalations are handled – not just what is escalated

- Celebrate examples of teams resolving issues constructively.

One leadership team introduced a 'de-escalation' round in their weekly forum. Each member shared a moment when their team had resolved a challenge independently. This simple ritual shifted the focus from problems to progress – and built confidence across the system.

Creating space for recovery

Sometimes, the only way forward is a reset. This doesn't mean stopping the project – but it may mean pausing certain behaviours or assumptions.

I once worked on a project where the team had grown quickly, communication had become formal and brittle, and performance had slipped. When a milestone was missed, senior leadership stepped in – not to assign blame, but to support a reset.

The project paused for two days. Teams met face-to-face. Expectations were clarified. Priorities were reset. Behavioural norms were agreed. The tone shifted. And the programme got back on track.

Not every reset needs to be dramatic. But all teams need moments to stop, reflect and reorient. Otherwise, drift becomes dysfunction.

So what? Over to you...

1.   Where do I see signs of a team that's stuck –
     not just stressed?

2. How could I help surface difficult truths – and what's being left unsaid?

3. What small shift could unblock energy, trust or clarity in my team?

Day 10

Embedding a learning culture

In a Big Team, learning cannot be an afterthought. It must be built into the way the team works – from individual habits to system-wide routines. Learning is how we adapt, improve and stay resilient in the face of complexity.

The need for continuous learning in complex team environments

Most people working on projects would agree that they learn more when working in a high-pressure team than they do sitting in a classroom or taking an online course. The problem is that we are usually too busy doing the work to actually process the learning.

Learning is too often viewed as something that happens in hindsight – through a lessons-learned review at the end of the programme. The trouble is that very few people are interested in reading a report from a project that they did not work on.

In complex projects, this traditional approach is no longer enough. The pace of change, the scale of interdependence and the unpredictability of challenges require learning to happen in real time.

The best Big Teams are learning systems. They continuously adjust. They reflect as they go. They share insight across boundaries and they treat every issue as an opportunity to improve – not just react.

In one programme, every major milestone was followed by a 30-minute 'learning loop'. These short reviews involved the people who had done the work – not just managers. The key question was 'What surprised us, and what will we do differently next time?'

Over time, these loops reduced repeated mistakes, accelerated onboarding and improved planning accuracy.

Creating feedback loops, after action reviews and collective sense making

A simple technique for creating a culture of learning is the After Action Review (AAR). First developed by the US military, the AAR is a structured process for reflecting on what happened, why it happened and what can be learned.

The key principles are:

- Involve the people who were directly engaged
- Focus on facts and behaviour, not blame
- Capture insights quickly while they're fresh
- Share findings in accessible, usable ways.

One project I worked on held short AARs after every major milestone. These were run at the team level, supported by facilitators. Each AAR generated three key insights, which were shared at cross-team forums. Over time, this built a shared knowledge base – and a habit of reflection.

Learning also happens through informal reflection: corridor conversations, coaching questions, cross-team check-ins. Leaders must make space for these and model the behaviour themselves.

Some teams use visual management tools to make learning visible – like 'What We've Learned' boards in shared spaces. Others run short 'pause and reflect' huddles at the end of the week.

The method matters less than the routine. If reflection is rare, learning is slow. If reflection is regular, learning becomes part of how the team thinks.

Building a team culture that evolves and improves over time

Big Teams are temporary, but the lessons they generate can be long-lasting – if they are harvested properly. More importantly, teams that learn in real time are more adaptive, resilient and capable of delivering in complex environments.

The foundation of a learning culture is psychological safety: people must feel free to admit mistakes, share uncertainties and ask questions.

The accelerant is routine: learning must be part of the way the team works, not an occasional event.

The proof is in the shift: when teams begin to ask, 'What did we learn?' as naturally as 'What's the deadline?', you know the culture has changed.

In one infrastructure project, the leadership team embedded learning moments into their reporting. Every update included three components: status, risk and learning. Teams were expected to share one insight – good or bad – from the last two weeks. This shifted attention from delivery alone to delivery with awareness.

This didn't slow the work down. It made it smarter.

When learning becomes the norm, teams don't just perform – they improve.

Enabling learning across boundaries

In Big Teams, learning is not just individual or local. It must travel across teams.

To support this:

- Capture learning in usable formats – not just reports, but short stories, tips, templates, diagrams
- Share learning in places people already visit – stand-ups, forums, newsletters
- Recognize those who share insights, not just those who hit targets
- Connect people who've solved problems with those facing them now.

One programme created a simple 'insight of the month' spotlight, shared across workstreams. It featured a short story of how one team solved a challenge. These stories became conversation starters and source material for others.

Another project created cross-team learning sprints – two-day sessions where representatives from different teams came together to tackle shared issues. The aim wasn't just to fix problems – it was to build collective sense-making and accelerate shared understanding.

Teams that learn together grow stronger together.

Learning as leadership practice

Leaders who foster learning don't just ask for updates. They ask reflective questions:

- What's surprised us recently?
- What do we understand better now than we did last month?
- What are we pretending not to know?
- What do we want others to learn from this experience?

These questions change the tone of conversation. They make it okay to be uncertain. They reveal hidden insight. They support a culture of growth rather than perfection.

Leaders must model this mindset. If senior leaders never admit mistakes, no one else will. If leaders don't pause to reflect, teams won't either.

In a learning culture, the best ideas don't just come from the top. They emerge from interaction – when people are free to notice, test, share and adapt.

✏️ So what? Over to you...

1. How do we currently capture learning – and is it influencing decisions?

---

2. Do people feel safe to reflect, admit gaps and ask questions?

3. What routine could we adopt this week to embed learning in our delivery?

Conclusion

Working with Big Teams is demanding – but deeply rewarding. It requires shifting how we think about leadership, structure, relationships and learning. And above all, it asks us to take human behaviour seriously.

Big Teams are a necessary feature of modern society. As the demand for complex infrastructure and technological solutions continues to grow, so does the need to bring together the talents and efforts of many people, often from different organizations and disciplines. Our ability to work effectively in Big Teams is therefore a key determinant of future progress.

This book has attempted to shine a light on the elements that help create successful outcomes. These include building a clear purpose, paying attention to team dynamics, creating effective structures for collaboration, supporting distributed leadership and embedding learning into everyday work.

There's still much to learn. The research I've carried out has identified many factors, but it's also revealed how much is context dependent. What works in one team may not work in another. The ability to tune into what is happening within and between teams is therefore a core skill for leaders of Big Teams.

I hope that the importance of deliberate design has come through loud and clear. Teams rarely become high performing by accident. The behaviours, structures and expectations that support success must be intentionally created, consistently modelled and actively maintained.

Another key theme is the role of learning. Projects operate under pressure. Mistakes will happen. Unexpected challenges will arise. The question is not whether we can avoid these – but whether we can learn from them fast enough to adapt and improve.

Big Teams thrive when there is:

- Psychological safety to speak openly
- Clarity about purpose and values
- Trust between individuals and teams
- Shared leadership and mutual accountability
- Space and time to reflect and learn.

These are not 'soft' factors. They are central to delivery in complex environments.

Conclusion

I hope this book has given you some practical insights, some useful models, and some questions to explore with your own teams. Whether you are leading a team of 20 or 2,000, the same principles apply: people need to feel connected, respected and aligned.

If you take away only one thing, let it be this: success in Big Teams depends on the human system working well. You may have the best tools, the smartest strategy and the most detailed plan – but if people don't talk to each other, trust each other and work together, none of that will matter.

My invitation to you is to stay curious. Observe your team, ask different questions, try new routines, support others in leading well.

The future will not be delivered by lone heroes. It will be built by teams of teams – learning, adapting and succeeding together.

Let's do the work.

Endnote

[1] In J. Katzenbach and D. Smith, *The Wisdom of Teams* (1993), p. 45.

Enjoyed this?
Then you'll love…

Big Teams by Tony Llewellyn

This is a book about working with large teams of people. Whether your team involves 30 people or 3,000, the organizational dynamics are significantly different for a project manager used to dealing with smaller teams. As the project scales up in size and complexity, the processes and skills required change. As project leader, your focus moves from the technical aspects of project delivery to enabling, facilitating and integrating the different sub-teams into a cohesive whole.

Big Teams examines the research on team dynamics and the latest thinking on leadership in a project or programme environment. It features stories and case studies based on interviews with project leaders from a range of major projects and programmes.

Structured around three core themes – Alignment, Engagement and Resilience – it gives you invaluable, practical guidance on setting up and running an effective team of teams.

As with all Tony Llewellyn's books, *Big Teams* is written in an accessible style with the focus on real-world application, but the academic underpinning is rigorous and will be a useful reference for any student studying project leadership.

Other 6-Minute Smarts titles

Building Great Teams (based on *Workshop Culture* by Alison Coward)

Collaborate Better (based on *Collabor(h)ate* by Deb Mashek PhD)

Customer Success Essentials (based on *The Customer Success Pioneer* by Kellie Lucas)

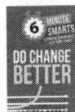

Do Change Better (based on *How to be a Change Superhero* by Lucinda Carney)

Find Your Confidence (based on *Coach Yourself Confident* by Julie Smith)

Get That Promotion (based on *Getting On* by Joanna Gaudoin)

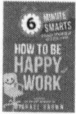

How to be Happy at Work (based on
My Job Isn't Working!
by Michael Brown)

How to Get to Know Your Customer
(based on *Do Penguins Eat Peaches?*
by Katie Tucker)

The Listening Leader (based on *The
Listening Shift* by Janie Van Hool)

Mastering People Management (based on
Mission: To Manage
by Marianne Page)

No-Nonsense PR (based on
Hype Yourself by Lucy Werner)

Present Like a Pro (based on
Executive Presentations
by Jacqui Harper)

Reimagine Your Career (based on
Work/Life Flywheel
by Ollie Henderson)

Sales Made Simple (based on
More Sales Please
by Sara Nasser Dalrymple)

The Speed Storytelling Toolkit (based on
Exposure by Felicity Cowie)

Stay Focused (based on *Attention!*
by Rob Hatch)

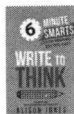

Write to Think (based on *Exploratory
Writing* by Alison Jones)

Look out for more titles coming soon! Visit
www.practicalinspiration.com for all our
latest titles.